Between Stations

Between Stations

Andy Willoughby

smoke STACK BOOKS

Smokestack Books
1 Lake Terrace, Grewelthorpe, Ripon HG4 3BU
e-mail: info@smokestack-books.co.uk
www.smokestack-books.co.uk

ISBN 978-0-9931490-6-1

Smokestack Books is represented
by Inpress Ltd

Between Stations

*For Lempi in memory of all the times
your father has saved my life
(and vice versa).*

For Kalle and Esa – my brothers in eternity.

From Middlesbrough to Saltburn past Coatham Marshes
as early winter comes sweeping in today from Siberia.
Restless snow flurries start to obscure looming shapes –
the final historical remains of ironworks, steel mills,
stranded black locomotives that pulled the smelt in pigs
from weary morning to never-dark childhood night,
to be converted into steel that still spans the globe.
Abandoned buildings, that still spew out smoke
in my attic-stored adolescent sketch books,
haunt the eye like shells of bombed cathedrals.
This was all marshland once; hidden slag-heaps
lie under grass covered bumps lining the sides
of trickling inlets of the Tees with its metal cranes:
intricate insect totems poke their heads at the North Sea.
Giant deer, elk and other ancient mammal bones
dissolved into this bleak beauty by the estuary:
through whirling flakes you can see them still.
Easy too, to see the Conqueror lost in fog here
only a few feet away from Northern swords
sending Norman soldiers to their long grave
but the thick sea mist that cut him off saved his neck:
no resistance then could stop the North's razing
and now no entreaty too could save the Salamander
in the lone blast furnace: the fiery heart – last survivor
of the hundreds that lined the river banks an age ago,
making this the land of dragons with satsuma skies
welcoming the Welshmen who came to Eston mines,
recent death by neglect the final chapter of the onslaught
begun back then by the blunt headed warrior king
they cared to name our next Prince of Wales after.

I finger my faded neck scar where the tumour was
and meditate upon the random nature of survival
of peoples, of kings, of dreams, of fragments of memory
and this train becomes another one over a decade ago.
Window blur of winter bleak and re-hashed history
takes me back to the vistas from the Siberian train
when, in silent moments I looked into endless forest
passing by in flashes of Autumn gold and silver birch:
felt cold fear that stretched back beyond our time,
conjured up the masses transported past those trees,
and compromised poets punished for incorrect lines
looking over the steppes to the edge of the forest,
looking for the Baba Yaga's chicken legged house –
oh to be caught in it running away into the pines!
Hungry skinny witches preferred to slow gulags.
You slowly revolve what sent you there: chance chain
ricochet from London heartbreak to the shores of Suomi
to the Far North and windswept steppes and the shaman
of the Khanty who told us *the hour of the wolf is at hand.*
At Helsinki station at the trip's outset I knew nothing
of the tribes of the North, just chancing it on instinct
that something there would stitch the wound I'd been
worrying at for years, some vision would restore me
beyond the state of defiant ursine roaring to calm.

In Turku I ate *karhunliha*, the flesh of my familiar:
bumbled and stumbled like a half mad circus bruin
sleeping down in the cellar of my old friend's house,
drank through panic attacks, began to meet the cast
of the northbound trip, that endless locomotive hurtling.
I wildly fancied eating bear in a restaurant would fix
the holes of broken relationships, years of wandering,
constant weeks of separation from my young child,
and it seemed that the soothing salve of friendship too
had brought me back to some innocence, some *seeing*
that happened at that moment the ice broke on the
Aurajoki that Easter morning and the black icy lump
broke inside me, but the healing was incomplete:
I could not make love my own season though spring
sent me the unearned gift of a welcoming girl, the dark of
the market town, the weight of the past, unquenchable thirst,
kept me stumbling full of appetite and rage, making every
offer of a home like the tormenting doors of a cage.

So when once upon a summertime's third day's drinking
in mid-festival floating with minds beautiful and far away,
a lost poet with flowing hair offered to take me to Siberia
for Fenn-Ugrian congress of course I growled an affirmative.
In this little hometown train carriage I ponder my choices
wonder if it was random chance or some norn-woven web
that always said solid blonde Kalle and wild wanderer Esa
were meant to be the poles at the extremes of my journey;
the three of us surrounded by the other travelling writers
a triangular conundrum in a circle at the centre of a puzzle
I'm still seeking to solve, wild men, clown seers, holy fools
the drinkers of fire and milk, salt sucker truth seekers
suspended but still moving in the eye of Blake's eternity
in the land of strong vodka, white tigers and great bears.
The marsh here, nestled between the busy road to Redcar
And the murdered furnace, contains its own totems:
the swan, the frog, the hunched monkish grey heron,
the blizzard obscures them but they are memory-solid
and are eternal as they are short-lived. The dark tower
in the distance once held that precious fire breather,
the molten core beast that needed constant feeding
as sharp beaks of vicious speculators hovered above
as deadly as the heron with about as much compassion.
It was the last of its kind and the people here know it.

We are all proud of the Dorman Long signs on tracks,
girders and bridges studied on travels, that confirm for us
that these towns have made their mark though we know
too well that blood and sacrifice paid for our identity tags:
legends of fallen lads pushed down into the furnace smelt
by their own grim fathers to end their molten sufferings,
400 men and boys crushed and broken in our mines,
with their cathedral height shafts and heavy rock falls.
Who are we now without our steel? Nationalist graffiti
sprayed on house walls and the distant flag of St George
planted at the top of the iron drained hills in a game
of put-up-to-be-taken-down, put-up-again-to-be-taken-down,
begs the question of where we came from in these towns.
Long ago there was only a line of small villages here
in swampy grass filled bogland with a coast of giant cliffs,
after bronze age tribes and millennia of small farms
raided and settled by viking invaders who left their
legacy in names of places that Danish visitors recognise,
and some hidden in transformations: from Odin's Berg
to Roseberry Topping, sacrificial mound to summer idyll,
the ferric seam magnetised them: haphazard pilgrims
Celts and Saxons, Welsh, Cornish, Irish, Scots and Geordies
Yorkshire folk, Norfolk exiles, Christian, Sikh, Jew and Muslim.

Where are the tribes of Siberia's far north now I wonder
as the industries that spawned us here have taken away
and destroyed their own sacred lands, brought strangers
desperate for some work to outnumber them by the million,
whilst we dolefully mourn work's gradual withdrawal here,
count the cost in benefits and workless agony of dead fires?
Can it be what sustained us for so long has destroyed them?
The stock still grey heron's growing too big in my mind's eye
I don't want to think of the sinister totem birds of Den Haag
that haunted me horrendously after the death of my mother,
and flapped towards me again as I waited for the removal
of the ominous neck lump I sensed must be a malignancy,
and spread its wings over our marriage bed as seas raged
down the winter sea front outside our Amber Street window.
It's much better to think of what was survived once long ago;
more than ten years gone since we rioted north before the snow,
a comic book version of *Kalevala* with an extra clown in tow.

That night you threw dice that came up Khanty Mansisk
You'd been drinking away the days with Esa Hirvonen,
pondering the significance of his name: why would
Jesus of the Elk have been sent to you as a compadre
if you weren't meant to see something in the wilds?
Why had you met Kalle the storyteller outside the Alko
that time if you weren't meant to need his rocky strength
and his absurd wit to temper your wild flights of fancy?
You didn't know one day you'd be godfather to his child –
but predestination is not a belief I can easily sign up to.
There is only the present, I chanted as the waves rolled
that day when I got the diagnosis of three death spots,
dark multiple headed dragon I foresaw and faced down
with a grizzly roar during a meditation spirit vision,
all that matters is how we handle this coming wave:
that one now – breaking loud on the Cleveland coast –
the one you throat-sing as it breaks into surf for the shore.
Joe Strummer was right I hoped, the future is unwritten,
physics tells us there is no future in the now, just future*s*,
moved to by accident or design: I could have disembarked
after all in Petersburg or Moscow and stayed there for good
could have opted not to go to see my doctor in time,
ignored my wife's concerns and let the lump further ripen,
found out the true meaning of that beautiful word metastasis,
could have backed out of Ville's offer made down the phone
I could have been *Billy Liar* and stayed unsafe at home;
(That film made as many choices as *On the Road* for me
I'd never be the one to turn down the trip with Julie Christie.)
My heads packed full of this stuff: on a red brick estate
it's all you can build your eventual escape routes from;
the lucky detritus of art and culture fallen from the table,
just enough inspiration to keep going, to see it through –
the loneliness of the long distance poet, *Sisu* in Finnish
tempered by poetry, comedy, punk, flashy shards of rock'n'roll.

In his first incarnation Esa was a young handsome man
in leather pants touched by the shade of Jim Morrison.
At his second coming he was a fat wild Hawaiian shirt
throwing around his money like it was catching fire,
escaping the poetry bum's life on the back of a lucky win
split with him by his habitually inebriated father,
in the third incarnation he had grown a prophet's beard
was running out of cash and had become whip thin
his hair was down to his ass his teeth were turning black;
whatever the changes our friendship soon came back.
Elk and bear in a drinkers' waltz of turned over tables
carved long ago on the underside of a sacred stone.
The kind of man who'd invite you to go to Siberia
in a post festival downtown downbeat shady green bar
after three days of binging on black underworld potions,
caught in the surging ebb and flow of his runo days
with malt whisky and beer chasers beginning to kick in
with the growling literary conversation never diminished;
your slowed down Boro gabble, his ponderous deep drawl:
Jesus of the Elk, whose light glows electric blue,
like it does whenever he steps out onto a stage,
as you drop a coin in the last jukebox, unleash
the MC5 : *Kick Out The Jams You Motherfuckers!*

But we both know we don't have too many jams
left to kick out now man, as we sink into the sea green
light of another day in the shady bar world discussing
the necessary relationship of ugliness to beauty
the hidden tenderness in the works of Charles Bukowski,
the ignorance of the critics and our developing plans
to get back into shape. The call comes and he tells you
It's Ville we have plans to travel to Siberia, you want to go?
Overcoming trepidation, thinking of manic Neil and Jack
you shout *vamanos compadre* let's go let's go (oh no),
you realise you will have to let your new love know though
that just after moving in together you'll leave her alone.
Once it's said there's no going back: the Teesside iron
in the backbone will sustain you far away from home:
chant now – *the smoke in the lungs and the fire in the bones,
the smoke in the lungs and the fire in the bones
the smoke in the lungs and the fire in the bones.*

Take Kalle too, my love says, always knowing more
of what is needed when I am blundering blindly
He knows stuff about travelling he'll keep you safe
I blustered then conceded though I remembered his tale
of how he sat on a nest full of biting insects in the jungle
and got his testicles infested but hey we all make mistakes.
Kalle, who knows of the territory from which I came
Kalle, of the Tampere aeroplane factory workers' estate
Kalle, with the viking hair and lifelong rocker's heart,
Kalle, with his sheds full of bits and bobs and motorbike parts
with his Nik Nak nickname and his minimalist poems,
says he cannot let me go without him so far from home
Kalle says *yes* Kalle says *let's go* Kalle says *did you know
the people of Khanty Mansisk have a secret golden woman
do you know she is supposed to sit on a flying saucer?
We have no choice but to try to track her down she knows
something we don't, you know Von Daniken was mad for her
she's got to be magical!* I hoped she'd heal me further,
calm this restlessness that throws me from town to town,
love disintegrating always unable to rest or settle down:
I will seek her and survive, will find a constant path
so I can keep holding it together as son, lover and father
through days of daily teaching toil and nights of temptation.
a half assed grail quest, in a haphazard bards' formation
to a place not even half formed in the shadows of my brain:
we were already on the train, were we *always* on that train?

I selected my companions from our new home randomly –
light travelling was desirable so only a slim volume of
Songs of Innocence and Experience (unillustrated)
a basic (useless) Russian Guide and Thubron's *In Siberia*
made it in my back pack with a tape of *Blonde on Blonde*
and my ancient battered walkman – already an antique
in that breath pause between cd player and smart device.
Billy Blake and Bobby began an immediate conversation
behind the veil and the little old white stolen book
started glowing in my ruck sack as soon as I set out.
Finally, stuffed in my back pocket a crumpled print out
of Ob-Ugrian folk songs in poorly rhymed translations:
a last minute desperate gesture to try to visualise
a people I'd never heard of, a place I'd never dreamed about.
My two amigos met me with the rest of the ensemble
in the cafe below the stone giants whose grand balls mark
the Helsinki departure point from one world to another;
Ville of the Fenn-Ugrian knowledge with his blonde beard
and the dome of his gleaming pate, champion of native rights,
Aki shape-shifter with sharp glasses and black leather coat,
with his experimental magazines of formal postmodern juggling,
and last came Rita of the red hair and rosy cheeks joining us
with her glasses and brimming plastic bags of paper notes
her dogged determination to find facts and her own human truth:
a ramshackle expedition that would have made Scott laugh.

In Moscow Kalle says *mmm yes it is a Trans-Siberian express*
but I must point out it's not THE Trans-Siberian express.
On board I think that the beach boys must be big here –
could it really be that Russians don't like the cold?
Even in September the train's heating blast dries the air
swelling inflamed sinuses so our gruff snores awake us
day and night in clanking train heading through the Urals
on the *platzenkartz* upper bunk I doze on, killing time,
as the steppes take over from suburban settlements
while William Blake sings '*weep* '*weep* in my back pocket,
it seems we have been travelling forever and ever and ever
like in that old Hammer film, its name now eludes me,
where Peter Cushing informs the costumed carriage
that '*Now all the tales are told you are on your way to hell!*'
caught in eternity by vibrations that shake our very atoms,
somewhere from out of time Osip Mandelstam is asking me,
So what did they send you here for? Don't believe it was just
Stalin's cockroach moustache with me, or the slimy hands,
I was done for a long time before that and saw it coming
did I ever tell you about the vision of the chopping block
deep in the woods – keep your eye out for it poet brother!
I shouldn't have to tell you it's still there one way or another,
the dark arts come in many shapes, sizes and political disguises.
What's that howling I murmur half un-asleep, Kalle says
take a blast on your inhaler man your asthma is singing
as yet another nose spray blast stings our sinuses open.

Suddenly fond memories of the train to St Petersburg,
where we had an almost private room shared for a while
with Kyril the curly haired convivial soft pornographer
breaking out his private stash of black label vodka,
showing us his wares with an open faced friendly smile
see this one here, the blonde centrefold with the very big tits
she looks nothing at all like this – it's all done with airbrush
theres no truth in her pretty face or any of her private bits
if you visit me though you can meet girls really like this!
Tawdry illusionist of technology and money making revolution
reminded us of falseness of appearance, elusiveness of truth,
that first train designed for comfort, the staff in blue uniforms
Super Hostess not blinking an eye when the elk messiah
unleashes a savage sneeze into the diner's ash tray
shortly after declaring over a stoli: *after all we must recognise*
we are now international gentleman, we must have some style!
Ash clung to Esa's Christ beard, making him a grey Pompeii
figure whilst we guffawed and snorted beer from our lout-snouts
he sat still and bewildered with man of constant sorrow eyes
hanging on to his lace thin dignity, as we pulled into Moscow
the waitress handing him a napkin with no hint of a smile;
a Russian Veronica clothed in the palest hue of the sky
offering him only stern succour as I contemplate Vlad Lenin,
avoid Kalle's eye, attempt to wipe off my conspirator's grin.

In the Moscow station in the new free market Russia
in the gaze of the marble eyes of Vladimir Ilyich Ulyanov
an old, old man slowly dropped his wooden stick
in the neon room looking over at the newly ironic statue,
how it clattered harshly on the cold marble cafeteria floor
as we drank hot watery coffee on arrival from Petersburg!
I imagined then he was dreaming of being a little boy
staring in wonder at the boiling crowds on Nevsky Prospect.
He awoke from February 1917 with a spasmodic jerk
his battered brown boots sent his stick wildly spinning
as he opened startled eyes to the sound of Abba singing
on the cafe radio; *'One of us is crying, one of us is lying'*
police sirens unnerved us on streets near red square
as rumours of exploding black widows of Chechnya
emerged from numerous half understood conversations
near the entrance to Lenin's tomb, their whoop followed us
into the silence of the orthodox church where I saw
pictures of the virgin as golden woman in glittering icons
offering some comfort to poor old weathered ladies immune
to all the years of atheist ideology, their faces long as rivers.
Every Muslim woman in the street that day transformed
into a potential bomb by the news as the old religions
carried on their work filling up everyone's shadow,
though I thought myself detached and likely to see
a passing black cat as just that, my thumb and finger
caressed the St Christopher mother gave me long ago
as we passed the heroes' murals of the Moscow Metro
and I remembered the Sunday candles and those stations
of the cross carried out in Lent, how the depths of her in prayer
silently threading the rosary beads through work worn hands
was a beautiful candle-lit sight in the days of childhood,
no matter what my education has given me, or taken away

At South Bank I get the smell of incense in my nostrils
instead of the pungent sulphur stench of brimstone
from the shut-down, silent coke ovens so familiar here.
All those thoughts of the religion that still haunts me
you have to ask yourself said sweet Sister Mary-Teresa
in any situation what would Jesus do? I once got off here,
just a ten minute walk from where I went to Catholic school,
shortly before they sliced out the lump and my thyroid,
and walked over the bridge the other way seeking satori
on the Smith's Dock Road, looking for clues in the overgrowth
from the wild undergrowth bursting through broken fences,
in the graffitti on the junkyard wall, in a discarded worker's glove,
a red tall poppy, swirls of barbed wire and an old circus poster
plastered to a fence where the shift workers would walk
in their booted thousands in the heydays of the shipyard.
Jesus would weep at the waste and celebrate the love
that helped the discarded survive and continue to just be,
I found myself thinking, despite the zen intention of my walk,
but now in this fold of locomotive time he cracks a whip
to the rattle of this threadbare train, condemns moneylenders
and his beard looks more like a neatly trimmed goatee.

I think of Paris, mourn the dead innocents of Iraq and Syria
worry at the nagging knowledge of Palestine's atrocities,
of course I then remember those moments in Moscow
when all women in Burkhas seemed like potential explosives,
worry about a world of projected shadows and hidden hands,
remember how it feels to be made the object of suspicion,
think the only path to the infinite is not defined in any text
but inscribed in the very atoms that make every human heart:
contemplate the wabi-sabi Buddha orange of worker's glove
I photographed against the dusty path where wildflowers
poked through the fence from the old steelworks' verge
dangling over the five fingers that have no need for hands
Baudelaire's *Terrain Vague* reversed; industry receding
the opposite of mineral and gas rich Siberian hinterlands.

Ville our reluctant leader calls us all to the Uralic train
as Sergei Eisenstein whispers in my ear: *check out this montage –*
of the steps from Potemkin to the old, old man's bleary eyes
opening to Agnetha and Anni-Frid still Top of the Pops
provoking from him a long heartfelt sigh, cut to them
singing the volga boat song and segueing into a chorus
of Money Money Money as next cut screens frozen homeless,
with their beards of frost and their winter hearts stopped,
getting zipped into bags in morgues in a few months' time
now the state has stopped cradling them in unwieldy paws,
next the attendants discuss the exploding Chechen widows:
the topic of today lingering in the near future day-mare feature
as we move sharply between the metallic tracks and lines
I try to show Sergei my forefathers in the trip's foundations
looking at the sleepers for the tell tale Dorman Long signs
before we are transported by this otherworldly locomotive
over the distant mountains to where the golden lady shines.
Meanwhile Ville tells us of a recent spate of deaths of drinkers
who imbibed a concoction of paint thinner and cheap perfume,
and to beware of accepting any random stranger's hip flask,
lest it turn us all bad potato blind and deliver us to Dr Doom
while my mind takes in the brave new world of a Siberian train.

The track and train's rattle sounds just like balalaika music,
Kalle and Esa start singing *Kalinka, Kalinka, Kalinka Moloko!*
I hear them on a rickety soundtrack along with Dylan
intoning monotonously: *everybody let's get stoned*
on last century's stuttering battery-low sony walkman,
as I stagger like a sailor just arrived back on solid land
down the aisle, desperate to piss out Siberski Korona,
which we have supped monotonously now for millennia:
poor poets rich enough to sit all kalinking day in the diner
indigenous travellers avoid in favour of flasks and dry noodles.
We swing back and forth between beer and sips of vodka,
between fried eggs and small packets of dried squid flesh
between bottled water and little plastic cups of milk,
not enough Russian between us to order much else.
Esa plays inscrutable chess with Aki the master of forms
and Ville and Rita goof up and down in search of a new story,
spilling paper and sexual frustration in their spirit driven wake.
We drunkenly mutter *moloko, moloko, moloko,* the waitress sighs:
Kalle says *Mmm it's interesting, all the girls who work on this train*
look like models who have escaped from Hefner's Russian house
they don't need Curly Kyril's airbrush artistry. It's a good job here:
see they carry themselves with pride and ignore our hungry eyes.
Tell them who we are I exclaim: the New Molokovian movement,
not ordinary milk guzzlers but intrepid collectors of lost legends!
The ghosts of the electrification of the soviet union crackles
in the bones of their face croaks black clad '66 Dylan in my ear
as we all decide it's way past time to try to get a little shut eye.

Through my half-cut pupils the carriage matron's Brezhnev's wife
beetle browed, sitting stern and lumpen by the hot water boiler,
that sacred fountain of the long distance economy carriage.
Her pungent coffee masks the smell of ripe feet dangling,
protruding from the rows of public bunks that line aisles
of the carriage all down both sides in clusters of eight.
One travelling group, of an unidentifiable ethnicity,
exudes strangely the sweet sharp smell of Spanish lemons,
filling my mind with black Goya visions as I clutch my cock
and try to piss straight into the stinking toilet's hole
misquoting: *the dream of reason brings forth monsters*
as though the mantra will protect my threatened soul;
I'm worried about the silent man who breathes smoke
from out of the cancer hole in his prison tattooed neck
who stands between the carriages in a nicotine cloud
with the stare of one with absolutely nothing left to lose,
I'm glad I don't know the meaning of his jailhouse tattoos
each one a cypher for indignities suffered or atrocity enacted,
I'm unnerved by the little diamond faced cleaner who peers at me
there for mile after tree lined mile, her eyes a blank mirror
where typically I can't distinguish curiosity from hostility.

My unreturned smile sticks to my face like a strange mask
in the bleary eyed hungover stuffy nosed morning
as I flee for the safety and sanctuary of the Dining Car.
I tell myself it's not that the little red haired train maid
hates you for being English and strange, it's just a different way;
remember the time you taught Russian kids English
all those years ago in faded picture postcard Scarborough?
How their mums pinned you like a butterfly with their eyes
after every session and you were surprised when complaints
didn't come into the boss that your sessions weren't serious –
there was too much laughter for learning to be going on,
the invitation that came to only you at the summer's end:
our children love you we want you to join us for a drink
how their smiles suddenly lit you up at the hotel table
drinking vodka and lemonade slammers with twenty mams
and a burly man who turned out to be their choir leader
how surprised they were that you'd read Pushkin and Tolstoy
more so that you could quote Dostoevsky and Mayakovsky
how they serenaded you in heavenly Russian voices
with folk songs and classics, a music hall perestroika
a few years after the Berlin wall had fallen, Yeltsin days,
hear them now those lovely mamas, quell your paranoia for a while;
it's ok to stare when you are unsure of what you're looking at,
you convince yourself and resolve to keep trying the smile.

Towards Redcar a skipped heartbeat makes you fear the fear
for a second, employ breathing strategies, empty the dark spots
out through the palms of your hands, consider the eternal
in the drifting soon-to-melt snowflakes, first fall of the year,
wonder how a haphazard journey feels now, reconsidered
in the light of post big C days, figure the same strategies apply:
deal with the now, carve out a little non-thinking time, focus
your eyes away from lines of pine after shrinking pine, realise
the train full of poets is one of the memories used to survive
when your head swam with the implications of part of you
already being dead inside, that eternity was there in every journey
if you used imagination's key to open up one of the spots in time,
that it was a gift to see your life move, not flash before your eyes.
Outside the window the dead forms of the steelworks' buildings,
that haunt you because they are more vivid in your mind's eye,
play their own music made of many layers of voices of forgotten men
who worked hard shifts inside to keep their children fed and alive,
but you cannot pick out any word to help a single voice survive.

You didn't know how to keep the fear beast from his feast
on the fast skips of the life pump in the days of the diner,
chess was not your game as you got another vodka down
on top of some fried eggs hoping the panic would subside
in thoughts of your lover's thighs while the room floated around.
Oh! shouts Mayakovsky from atop a dainty doily dressed table
Behold the rich variety of folk; from cities, from mountains
from plains and steppes, from villages and tower blocks
from all the hidden corners of this vast land mass
sleeping as one in their tiny beds hurtling through seasons
blindly, as you cross the Urals on this glorious machine
that links human to human like chain links of rhyme
Autumn turns more golden by the mile! Acceleration of time!
Winter gets nearer and nearer! Hear the starving wolf pack!
then his long figure with bloody hole in head deserts me.
Rolling on and on we go through unfathomable forests
of diminishing silver birch and pine and unnamed towns
beyond the legendary cities, with blank soviet era blocks
of dirty grey concrete with rooftop thickets of twisted aerials,
antennae pointing at the night sky trembling for the thrill
of the latest episode of a badly dubbed Brazilian soap.
Vlad's drowned out as the supermodel waitresses turn up the TV
in the rattling dining room now showing weird hybrids of rap
with skinhead gangster posers in leather shouting at me
it seems about trading my Lada for a sporty new something
Kalle says *they all look like young Vlad, these shorn rappers*
no longer a cloud in trousers – this vicious crowd in bling
rolling on and on we go as some glam pop star starts to sing.

Redcar: a bunch of rowdy auld lads stumble off singing,
bring me back to the now with a sudden whiff of danger
as they start to terrorise all my fellow passengers,
full of bitter and cheap shots stirred up by football failure,
sing about *eating hairy pie* and how they like to *hammer*
heads and *pile-drive into pussy,* fearful of emasculation
by redundancy, by benefits, they begin to proclaim old lyrics
about St George and how they'll not surrender to the IRA
ignoring the fact half of them will have Irish blood in them
and that they'd have a Turkish dragon-slayer deported
if he turned up now with his perishing kids on a rickety boat –
they need half understood symbols to keep them afloat,
it feels good to scream defiance to a perceived enemy
they've still got glasses in their hands I know full well here
how to keep my eyes not fully on them and freeze my face
in neutral, too weak from shifts in artificial thyroxine
to attempt to intervene, knowing well how the terrace thrill
can turn so quickly into threat, retreat into advance,
remember the kick of teenage freedom in numbers,
of adrenalin, being chased through streets and alleys
by the other tribe leading them to ambush where possible,
by the true hard knocks amongst this pack of gobshites,
how *I* feels better when it becomes *we,* know full well
that this doesn't always lead to solidarity but bloodshed,
still carry terrace rhythms in my head: a bass-line armoury
from the days before stadiums were full of families:
you're going to write your fucking poetry!
you're going to write your fucking poetry!

A Middlesbrough granny talks soft to her grandchild
trying to pull her frightened eyes off the ageing man-boys
from the fading frontline gang, she's too long in the tooth
to tell them to mind their ps and qs and the conductor's
staying well away to live to collect tickets on another day.
when they're gone she visibly relaxes, her stiff shoulders
lose the weight and the little girl talks about snowmen
while I remember the long years that passed by before
my daughter and I got to build one, when my weekend
and a snowfall at last coincided: *will we use old coal Dad?*
Yes we'll use coal love, carrots for a nose and carbon for eyes.
I recall my other protection on the *platzencartz* plunge:
the little blue photo album with precious pieces of frozen time
when my magical gift and me would Saturday adventure
along the shores and up the hills to rock pools and bilberries.

On the bunk below me a white haired babushka lies in bed
her little granddaughter sleeping opposite. Above, Kalle says
be careful getting down now don't dangle your balls man
over the narrow, hard bunk's raised edge, we are like
strange trolls living above this innocent little family.
It's interesting the fearsome figures of Russian mythology
and old folk tales may well be of Fenn-Ugric ethnicity
have you noticed how my classic Finnish upturned nose
is like a troll or elfs? And it's not difficult to see with his
long blonde hair hanging free how my mate's daughter
awoke once with two Finn bards in her house and told me
she thought the king of the elves and the king of the fairies
were crashing on their Middlesbrough living room floor.
Kalle says *of course most witches were just wise women*
with healing powers but here with their living shamanism
the Khanty and the Mansi would have been easy to other,
to see as demonic, Mansi built their houses on the marshes
on kinds of wooden stilts – easy for this to twist and turn in time
of crusade to the chicken legged house with the pot for children
on the dark edge of the forest, become the bone thin Baba Yaga,
of course this is just my theory, he whispers before dozing,
I wonder what the old lady makes of our strange faced bunch
our features carved from trees and pines and bogland peat,
try to figure how to reach out to them as my heart softens
to the breath of the little dark haired girl wishing she could
understand the funny stories about the dragon who eats toast
I'd made up for my own little Holly over the aching years,
even Esa with his Christ/Mad Monk hair and long bushy beard
stopping by on the way to fitful sleep notices the little one
carefully hides his pocket bottle and speaks softly, children
are not afraid of this mystic gentle man, prophet of doubt
who has told me frankly, sadly: *I am the alcoholic son*
of an alcoholic father – the father of a child I will not be.

Reading songs of innocence I hear William singing gaily
about the joy of the frolicking lamb and am carried off
into a dream world where the children aren't shoved down
mines and up chimneys and shot in school gymnasiums
or beaten at checkpoints, blown up in restaurants and concerts
bombed out of their own beds and nicknamed collateral,
caught in the money machine and the ensuing explosions
from the fall out of superpower's manipulating fanaticism
but my revery is broken when I shower the sweet granny
below with a cassette case, just as the yowl of the blues guitar
from *Blonde on Blonde* kicks in and I roll over carelessly.
I'm too flustered to remember the word for sorry in Russian
as she calls out in alarm, the little girl wakes sobbing hard,
worried that the weirdos are sizing her up for special soup.
Kalle dreams we are derailed or in a violent earthquake
sits up and smashes his forehead on the low train ceiling
and I am the evil wizard of the world of pandemonium.

In the morning I try to make amends, attempt conversation,
international relations as the carriage matron brews up,
I speak bad Russian, pull silent movie faces for the girl,
who looks half amused, half bewildered. I show pictures
from my blue album so they know I am father not monster:
I see the bruise darkening on the babushka's battered brow
as she inspects my wee attempts at human credentials
the little girl feeding ducks, the little girl in daddy's arms
amongst the grandiose gothic ruins of Whitby Abbey,
the little girl marking time blowing out tiny candles,
just as I'm beginning to feel our feet on common ground
she becomes confused at a Christmas picture of Holly
dancing, head adorned with a red pair of reindeer horns,
I get the feeling it looks like some kind of pagan ritual –
I mime and mumble *Rudolph, Father Christmas, Santa Claus*,
like some mistletoe clad mad escapee from a hospital
for the festively obsessed but am rescued by the arrival
of a Tartar man from the steppes clutching a live chicken
boarding the train in time to distract their attention –
the child and nanna smile with me at random poultry,
I feel my reputation restored as international gentleman
and retreat to the diner to talk about the terrible famine
following the failure of one of Stalin's five year plans;
or for some the success of his plot to pacify the Ukraine,
strange stories of cafés serving speciality of boiled baby.

At Longbeck we are well past the abandoned last furnace
and my thoughts shift to the kids I've seen in schools
this year whose dads used to work there, how Christmas
becomes a burden hard to bear when worlds of work
come crashing down, how we let children bear the weight
of poverty, how illiteracy is highest here in the whole country
how we once made so much wealth but have health rates
like some parts of the third world, how malnutrition and rickets
are returning, TB's not dead and homelessness is growing,
though the children of inheritance and the swelling super rich
are as blessed as the lucky child in that Billie Holiday song.
I have got the angry ranter's blues: *we woke up this morning
with our father's livelihoods dead, we woke up this morning
to news of the refugees fled, we woke up this morning
with attempts to shift the blame, we woke up this morning
to the same old bleeding game, we woke up this morning
to more of the same old same, I'm sick of the morning-mourning,
its time we saw who's really to blame* – but the greedy bankers
and their politicians sit impervious in the new walled city
talking about inevitability and the doctrine of non-intervention.
They are driving the workers out of the city with house prices.
William Blake said that brothels are built of bricks of religion
and that all the prisons are constructed with bricks of law
and now this is what we have all been working for: the few
clearing out the capitals driving the suffering out of sight
with invisible bricks of economy, deaf to the howls of the sick,
disabled and dying stripped of benefits by sanctimonious pricks
pontificating on shirkers, scroungers and hard working families
and tossing thousands more on the rigged market's scrapheap.
Is this deep rage within me what gripped Lenin's gut the day he
jumped out of the moving Tampere train to stay free? How can it
serve our small city with its existential motto *Erimus: we shall be?*
our ambition not to rule but to just be born and to survive.
We built the Empire, its railways, bridges and weapons of war,
what do they know of us in these corners hidden from visibility?
No train with first class carriages ever comes here anymore:
there's no Saltburn Spa or *Infant Hercules* for princes to see.

I begin to reflect again how some of those who lost their lives
to the iron from our own haunted hills that line this short route
held hopes once that Bolshevik ideals could free them too,
from their meagre existence in this boomtown hinterland;
near-slaves to the devouring Victorian furnace fires,
always kept in debt to the mine-owner's company stores,
their iron masters expanded into gross giants on profits
made from the world's desire for hard but malleable metal.
They walked up and out to listen to radicals like Shepard,
defied bosses' orders and sticks of the company guards while
long lines, many made like these below me from Teesside steel,
were laid into wilderness across the steppes and the great plains
opening for cheap whisky, smallpox and free enterprise –
swathes cut through peoples with suspect theologies:
Lakota, Dakota, Cheyenne, Kiowa, Apache, Crow,
Manifest Destiny on its iron horse brought death to buffalo.
In Siberia, our exported steel made alliance with slaughter
on a high speed locomotive named Historical Necessity –
ideology hid the relentless reaping of modernisation,
futurists praised machine, speed and sleek locomotion
as shamanic bones grew stark in the hidden graves,
steppe roamers were 'encouraged' into mines and factories,
Cossacks were commanded to swap horses for shining tractors,
roads and tracks advanced to the circle of the Arctic,
Khanty and Mansi seers joined Sitting Bull and Crazy Horse
in the broken circles of the ghost dancers' hoop,
those lost caretakers, not owners, of the precious land
where nature's spirit groans now beneath the whip hand
of all those who only believe in ever-growing production,
don't know Blake's wisdom of a world that can't be measured.

On his hard narrow bunk Kalle moans: a dreadful dreaming
of a young boy helplessly watching his mother pull away
on a train escorted by grim faced guards, gulag bound.
As we pass some dwellings improvised from big old oil barrels
thinking we are no longer in Europe anymore, that's for sure,
Esa Hirvonen starts twitching in nocturnal vodka withdrawal
he has fallen through a holy lovi again and become a bat
shapeshifter flittering and skittering through inky night air
serenaded by monk spirit with matching wild man beard
he turned himself into back on the outskirts of Yekaterinburg
and became, in the dining car, half jokingly, possessed by.
I join them then my fitful grim hangover kicking in, foresee
that on our eventual arrival in our undreamt of destination
I will stumble ursine and funky on civic reception dance-floor
Hirvonen the electric blue-light poet, AKA Jesus of the Elk,
will get his groove on as a manic cross between bat and fox
with a clutch of formidable Fenn-Ugrian/Ruski mammas
shaking his let-down tumbling prophet's hair apocalyptically
to the unlikely flashing disco's unrequested Boney M track
blaring out *'Ra Ra Rasputin lover of the Russian Queen'*
announcing through his long bible-crazy prophet beard
Yes, Yes I am Rasputin returned from the dead
to wrestle with the monolingual devil in Khanty Mansisk!

In the morning we are back at the table eating leather
patches of squid and more trackside vendor acquired salami
with some moloko to stop the sweats and shivers from sinus
infection and slow steady consumption of shots and bottles,
I do not know I have seen the future and don't believe in one;
I succumb finally to the challenge of the chequered board:
Esa plays chess often to still his suffering mind and soul
his hands shake still but he is so many moves ahead;
drinking will kill him one day he's aware of that: he says
in Udmurtia he heard the voices of the Fenn Ugrian dead
before he met his fox familiar in a mushroom style vision,
but there's heavy stuff that haunts him nipping at his heels
like Robert Johnson's relentless hell hound on the trail –
last night I saw his limbs twitching under bunk blankets
and swear he started drinking again in his sleep to stop it
his pocket vodka medicine response making me wonder
if this trip would tear us asunder, if we should all just bail
before the cost kicks in and our raging hearts fail
but as the vast steppes roll by in visions of endless grass
and the incredible shrinking Northern birches glow silver
in the sluggish rising sun's autumnal morning light
he demolishes my castles and captures my white queen,
his mind moves delicate through the mathematical spheres –
the board is no smaller than the whole of Russia for him,
like Mandelstam he seeks order from chaos with a classic move
I hear poor Osip applauding and Mayakovsky snort approval
as he brings down my helpless king to the level of a pawn
Old Blakie refuses advice, sneers the world can't be cut to size
that *the moves are not measurable you fool but infinite*
something my groaning opponent seems naturally to get
and gunslinger Dylan sings loud above the racket of the train
you're stuck inside this diner with the Albion Blues again.

The light's gone out in the sky at home, though when the snow clears
the stars and moon still shine, all Teessiders know that their worst fears
are realised as the spaces in between are now black not tangerine
from the furnace and the flare stacks, the shade that had faded to pale
since fiery childhood nights when flames burned along the banks
of the Tees, the auld boys down Dad's club used to tell me over beer,
you should have seen them skies when we were bairns there were veins
in the clouds glowing red we never knew the dark at all round here.
Now from this little train's window I note inky blackness, see spaces
between the stars and try not to calculate the distance from birth
to death thinking instead of Jesus of the Elk suffering on the tracks
when we disembarked at stops to stretch our legs and purchase sausage
from women of indeterminate age with each hard year etched on them.

Slicing the salami with a Swiss army knife to take with watery tea
brewed up with the carriage matron's rationed slow trickle
we talk about things that haunt us: the things we cannot change
the soldiers dead from his army service, the lovers out of range;
Esa has done his national service, hard to imagine him in uniform,
he once saw an armed carrier crash into the water full of men
and trap them all underwater, watched the bubbles rise then stop.
I think of my father and the friends he knew who died in training
crushed beneath a tank they tried to sleep under when rain came
and the man who got the rifle nuzzle rammed through his throat
from a sudden stop, how dad would yell at me if I held a cricket bat
the wrong way in front of me in the back seat of childhood cars
the things he'd seen but had never been able to write a poem about.
Esa sometimes carries a weight upon him that can't be shared
that disappears in his flaring electric glow when he hits the stage,
the aspect of the poet that cannot be seen in words on the page.
The page is all that's left of you whispers Osip Mandelstam
even if you left them only in the heads of others to be saved,
I think I have left and lost far too many in the recesses of my head
whilst working in thankless jobs or pissing it all up the wall
but the moment of the poet in the poem is eternal says Blake
I say nothing else thinking of how it sometimes seems to not be
something that you do but something that flows through you
sent from elsewhere to you to record and then to perform
how this is the talent that mustn't be hidden under the bush,
wonder if my courage would have held under a dictatorship
think about the shaman hiding out in the muddy swamps
to protect his golden woman, if she was in fact his muse
his spirit vision and not an object at all; immaterial, untouchable,
wonder where in his mind Mandelstam withdrew to in the camps,
if there was any hidden world of William's Los to shelter him
from the biting cold and bloodsucking lice and buckets of shit.
We crack a joke about the penalty for not drinking the tea,
talk about the poems we might perform at the destination,
I tell the lads their Teesside nicknames: Hirvo and Kalla,
wonder what poor Nannas will try to sell us at the next station.

Finally the train changes to another Northbound carriage
though in memory they are both amalgamated, similar
in the constant motion to the diner, though one thing remains
the hard eyed carriage maid bursting into a beautiful smile
as I bade her *dosvedanya* and she waved and waved and waved.
Later still , a spine-jarring bus from Pityak to Khanty Mansisk –
take a piss stop on rough roads, empty tins of tasteless beer
purchased at a station cafe by brave comrades Kalle and Aki,
look out over devastated cut down Taiga, and endless steppes at
the vast dark space lit by myriad oil, furnace and gas fires,
those familiar orange skies in a science fiction landscape
that also feel homely only to those of us from Middlesbrough,
as men transform open plains to get at buried, revered remnants:
prehistoric fauna is alchemical black gold and coal paid for in blood.
Esa reaches down and casually hands you a fossil from the floor;
quartz, shale and fragments of old bones scattered round our boots:
wonder how far you'd have to wander off this pockmarked road
to dig up the rotting human remains that the rough highway
and relentless tracks opening the far North were built on,
realise now the futility of the historical fools who invaded Russia.

Nearing Saltburn now, the sites of dead salamanders behind me
with nothing left to show of their fiery being, abandoned sites,
demolitions: remember the detonation dust at Grangetown that time?
The last shift you witnessed; entrancing shower of sparks and blazing river
from the tapped belly of the beast, directed by your old schoolmates
into the waiting pigs, how one told you of the beauty of it amidst the dirt,
how it hurt to think of men like that competing for jobs stacking shelves?
A town without its totem, only a football team to carry its name now:
Everywhere we go, people wanna know, who we are, who we are,
shall we tell 'em, yeah we'll tell 'em: we are the reds we are the reds...
But I know it's still iron and steel that somehow connects me to words:
in Finland the first time with a group of poets Kalle invited us to stay
at the site of an iron age fort at Voipaala; when I first opened Kalevala,
it was at Runo 10: the origin of iron, where the shaman Vainamoinen
must find the spell to stop the blood flowing fast from close to the bone,
the wound an axe has made, seeks the roots of the problem in the stone.
Remember the realisation as you got off the first Siberia train and Kalle
pointed out the Dorman Long sign on the railway sleeper? Recognition
that the tracks that bore you here really were from your hometown,
wonder what magical magnetism growing up beneath those iron hills
had seeped into your being, whether knowing these origins meant
that weeping wounds might finally be healed at our wyrd destination?

In Khanty Mansisk the centre all looks bright and newly built
the bridge with the arch like half a Macdonald's sign made elegant
by new gas money that's made its mark, our hotel is painted yellow
everything seems too shiny, the smell of paint and one or two
sticking out nails gives the impression that it was just yesterday:
they put it up to fool us, that the whole thing is a simulacrum
designed to trick us into not seeing the actual town, Kalle says
it's clear when we leave that they will take it all back down
but I wonder if they will ever return our passports, if we are on TV
on a new reality show for the rest of our lives entertaining Muscovites
as Ville tells us *come on down now for free drink and tasty bites*
at the welcoming reception in the modern hall across the way
we fools declare we'll just take one or two, take it easy for a day
before the conference opening we'll all be good citizens we say –
nobody told us about the Russians and the drinking games they play.
Kalle says *one vodka with the fish starter will probably be enough*
but then the endless toasts begin and the going's only for the tough.

The mayor toasts the town, we toast him then he toasts us all,
every few minutes another dignitary at his table slowly rises
to raise a glass to praise something about the brand new hall
or maybe another achievement, so many prizes washed down
with the clearest most pure stuff till every other table has a go
and the whole hall sings the equivalent of he's a jolly good fellow
in the nearby dance hall the DJ puts on Bony M and Jesus of the Elk
is really transformed into my dream of disco Rasputin; the night blurs
into a string of heartfelt greetings and bursts of hearty song
until the revellers begin to fade and we are joined by Mikhael –
the translator kodiak bear man with black beard who looks
like he should be carrying a machine gun in a violin case says,
well let's see how these Finns famously drink, laughing and pouring
as much booze as he can down the jolly English man, what
choice do we have but to make our stand to be the last ones standing?
Sure enough all the party crowd starts to fade away only we remain
the raggy-arsed poets and Riina who flew in with the famous authors
who tells me her first novel was about Black Sabbath loving rock chicks
and that Ozzie's yearning voice does something to her she can't describe,
and at our table two Khanty women with serene faces I don't recognise,
can't ethnically categorise, who don't drink, just nod a little and smile
so I can't help but see them almost as beautiful spirit guides,
wonder if they are actually with us or a trick of the fluorescent light
one tells me the other's name, says they are very interested in us,
outside under Autumn skies more full of stars than I have ever seen
adding to the dream feel of the moment telling me *Yulia wants you
to go with her, she has something she wants to show only to you*
I make a comment about being engaged, they shake their heads
disappointed it seems by my inference of an easily offered bed
rather than something of great import, it all slips away as the ceiling
spins in my shared twin room and I drift off into uneasy inner space
as Kalle says *maybe she was going to show you the golden woman's face?*
the morning brings confirmation of some karma in operation
but its hard to tell if its a punishment for evil or a reward for doing good,
I open my eyes in the twin room to a wall sprayed with goo and blood
Kalle says calmly *well you were choking to death on your own puke
I couldn't wake you so rolled you over then slept: that was a bit of luck!*
It's not the first or last time one of us will save the other's life.

43

On the last leg of my homebound winter trip to the raging coast
I am now settled in, anticipating warm hands and tenderness of foot
on foot in the North wind lashed night, I ponder all the secrets
I can never know, the truths or lies of past broken relationships,
the family matters taken to the grave with grandparents schooled
in the sudden shift of subject and the use of the tight pursed lip,
of what lies beyond the moment of contemplating breaking of the sea
decide it's enough that my woman of gold will be sleeping next to me
for one more night at least in a time when unsteady weather has torn
the roof off the building just around the corner and the rumble grows
ominously for yet another bombing, yet another war on terror,
know if we make fear our enemy then thats all that we can be –
every stranger, every shadow, a threat to our homeland security,
every minute of the one journey will get emptied of the sacred joy
of old Blakie's imagination, every grain of sand a suspect device
not the tiny gate way to the infinite, the touchstone of eternity,
I refuse to let them countdown my time on earth, those murderers
or those time servers: those false leaders who don't know the worth
of a lover's breath you listen to on sleepless nights as it mingles
with the eternal rocking of the raging white horse winter sea,
I begin to rethink the meaning of the motto *we shall be, we shall be*
remember the day I looked out over ten thousand miles of steppes
into the taiga on the horizon and felt Blake's Tyger looking back at me.

The whole conference feels like a dream I had on the Siberian train:
I wonder if all of everything since is still part of the fantasia arising
from the rattle of the tracks outside Pityak, it's time soon to hold a stone
in the palm of the hand gathered from Saltburn's old smuggler's shore
so its heft can outweigh memory, hold down the moment as alone
not just part of the flow; I remember meeting Riina Katajavuori again
in the elevator on the morning of Fenn Ugric conference, me and her,
after the toasts of the night before, missing our children with her baby
only recently born, we measured our distances in the same non-language
of the loss of time with the beloved, forged our friendship on quest cost,
the price you pay, talked about the natural etymology of our names
how hers translates as *juniper mountain* and mine *by the willows* –
that elevator journey is as long-lasting as the whole locomotive rush,
our friendship's foundation stone, solid below the decades, holding
up well still, pulsing a magic on all the stages we have since shared.

At the packed lecture theatre everybody's mood went giddy but mine –
I had a new name: *Willaboo Andy, Chairman of the British Delegation*.
There was a Union Jack on the stage, I was a panel member
representing the whole nation: the Finns laughed in the audience
till they fell off their chairs, as I sat there, hungover-dishevelled-desperate
for a morning beer, trying to not draw attention to myself, bluffing it
I thought as I hit the panel's translation button, holding it down
wondering why all the gang were exploding in unsurpassable mirth
at Willaboo; the last in the long line of great British clowns:
Charlie Chaplin, Stan Laurel and Mr Bean really had nothing on me
as I kept pressing the button for close up on the huge conference screen
Kalle says *I will always see your face up there on a giant tv dripping
beer sweat panic as the speeches go down the line like in a dream
you have when stressed about being naked, not being ready*, though
I started to blah blah about research into myth, nation and identity
and convince the audience that my strangeness was national eccentricity.
I'd just shifted into the familiar persona I always access to be able to teach
and relax when Ville tells me *tomorrow you get to deliver a lecture:
what will it be on?* Now you tell me about this you fucking moron!
I almost blurt but mumble on ethno-futurism echoing aspects of Yeats
Kalle says *yeah, just talk about that stuff, read a poem we've translated
Esa and I will perform with you, it will be a chance to shine, we'll be great*.

All the comic memories are coming back to me and I laugh out loud
for a second, the last passengers for Saltburn now glance across at me
assessing the possibility of insanity but decide I'm probably just wasted
though I'm sober and playing on my i-tunes for the sake of those times
Dylan's *Most Likely You Go Your Way (and I'll Go Mine):* esoteric knowledge
makes my guffaw subside to some kind of mysterious knowing smile
recalling the wise men my fool self met in a town somewhere out of time.
Rock Tree Boy is my Kiowa name said the Native American writer
who sat like a mountain at the far end of the international panel.
He knew I was half-blagging but liked my poem about shamanic
consumption of the flesh of the bear, told me his spirit familiar
was also ursine, and explained to me the need for the song of apology.
They sang to the bearskin at the head of the table for days you know!
I realised then why my healing still had so many thousand miles to go
I had been desperate but not revenant, revolving this outside the hall
I bought a leather charm of an elk leaping amongst the stars and moon,
The Khanty shaman told me *there is a wolf coming who will consume*
the silver light, now is his hour and he will try to eat all our languages.
Thoughts of shut down newspapers, dead journalists and new censorship
takes the smile from my twelve-years-later face as Dylan groans the lyrics
to his *sad eyed lady of the lowlands* and the knowledge of constant war
and the blood stained colour of oil seeps through all the years between
as the tiny diesel train slowly moves towards the off-white Pease bricks
of Saltburn's Victorian railway arches, a town built on industrial profit
by one of the sons of the first masters of rail, steam, iron and coal,
recall the story: how Henry claimed he saw a jewelled town on the cliff
in a silent Quaker vision and made building it the mission of his soul.

The Golden Woman is what the Khanty people saw, sat on a giant disc
there's a statue in the town now, it's said the secret police couldn't find her,
surviving shaman spirited whatever she was away to hidden swamps.
Under the memorial to her power we pose and cavort, find some craic
about flying saucers and desire for Amazonian goddesses from outer space
but secretly I looked at the serenity the artist put in the image of her face
remembered Fatima, Bernadette and Lourdes and revolved old thoughts
about the female power of the universe, remember how it's easier to pray
to or via a woman's image, think about the sensitive eyes of Jesus Christ
in renaissance paintings and tacky memes and the masculinity of Soviet
propaganda where strong worker women bulge with muscle and purpose
equipped with biceps and iron will, drive tractors and smash fascism,
trying to conjure an image in my mind's eye without preconception
or immaculate conception isn't easy in a Catholic shaped male brain:
'Hail Queen of heaven the Ocean Star, guide to the wanderer here below...
mother of Christ star of the sea, pray for the wanderer pray for me.'
She's still on my mind the golden woman, the idea she's in all women,
all the women I have known and failed, the woman I love now back home
and in me too if I learn to listen, in the forests and by the running streams.

Marketplace beer and translation workshops interrupted spirit dreams
but a woman's Russian accented voice is in my ear, a tug on my arm
in the coffee break, *we'd like to abduct you* she laughs, *let's quickly leave*
and this time I abandon caution and head for the door casual and calm:
she says she's an English teacher, she wants me to read at her college,
she hasn't asked for permission or filled in the necessary paperwork.
I feel like a pacifist James Bond; her assistant is a hulking Tatar man
who tells me his Anglicised name, something like Peter or Dan
it's not real but he feels good telling me the moniker he picked out,
you go on instinct, decide to trust again in the power of saying yes
though it often closely shaves you and drops you on strange shores
you are in the float with these new faces keen to show the hidden:
the town on the wrong side of the tracks not on the official tours,
small wooden dwellings for the workers and the people of the Steppes
no longer roaming nomads: houses contain and sanitise, homogenise
the cultures, bring small comforts though we are not in the central town
with its new hotels, we are in the same struggle you can find anywhere
of keeping the roof over children's heads, of just trying not to go down,
we are not so very different anywhere when you really look around.

I read to teenage kids and answer their shy questions as a rare curiosity,
talk about the futility of war and the fact that I too read Dostoevsky,
that Russian classics are actually in all our city libraries back home
that I read them alongside the beats as a culture starved teenager,
we do call and response slam poetry till the teacher tells me time to go.
Peter/Dan secret Tatar-name man asks me what would you like to see?
I tell him I'm interested in the places and tales of the Khanty and Mansi
he says he'll take me somewhere western tourists don't often get to be,
we drive to the hill where the Ob and Irtisch rivers meet far below,
making one mighty stream to flow into the circle of the Arctic;
easy to see a river of souls going back to Cossack invasions, Roman
explorers, ancient times in the river basin when the game was plenty
when the fish traps were full and belief in the cycles of nature held sway,
the teachers tell me *now you have to see the tower, it's at the highest point,
it's a steel replica of a Khanty tent* I remember my New Molokovian jest
as they tell me it's called a churn not a teepee, its shining metal sides
seem so unnatural on the forest surrounded peak: impossible to explain
the sudden sense of the familiar I felt before I asked for information,
the answer gave me clues, so far from home but on another iron leyline,
this was ferric country, the mines below my feet like the ones from home.
Stalin gave the native people *'productive'* lives beneath us in vast caverns
and the monument is a grotesque tribute to their former nomadic lives.
There's a glass lift in it, we ride it to the top like an inverted miners' cage,
at the top I look out, not to the inviting North Sea of child memory,
not to the seven sisters of local legend or the purple heather tint of moors,
but to the endless flat plains of bogland and steppes, ten thousand miles
and a million years of something stretched to nothing understood,
to the point of insanity by sheer vastness of the plains, endless horizons.

At Marske with its ancient Viking name you can see from the train to the sea;
I have looked for hours at the waves, it's a Cleveland boy's common dream
to glean ideas of adventure, James Cook grew up here, before the iron seam
was uncovered, lizard tail in the Saltburn cliffs, vast body in the hills near me
that drew the struggling masses to pick away at in cathedral size holes.
At the hill fort's circle, by the nab I imagined the yearning to travel beyond,
of men who in winter never saw the sun, starting their shift before it rose,
walking home in the treacherous dark on muddy paths pricked at by gorse
the sea for them then was just silver ripples of moonlight in their eyes.
In Siberia I thought how men below had not so long ago roamed the wild
what a soul cage they entered to keep up with the plan for a new world!
I knew as I looked across the plains too the foolishness of Napoleon
and of Hitler, here in Eurasia a thousand battalions could die in winter
west of the Urals they empty the cities and hide in this vast unknown
waiting for their allies: the ice and snow giants, to deal a devastating blow.
I felt the panic rising and breathed deep to get myself under some control,
a man could disappear here, brushed out of time like Blake's little fly
in a space like this it's easy to see how millions of humans could die:
as many people as there are years in the making of an oil field,
and still the land would remain blank and impervious without a tongue
its hardy grasses growing, its relentless life cycles going on and on,
then I remember to stop measuring, consider how land and people
are not really separate but one and understand the bear apology song
is not to one animal but to all the wilderness complete in one being,
see fear is overcome with love and common feeling, connection with
Russia, with Siberia, with the teachers and the myriad dead below
this moment, where terror became an ecstasy I cannot describe,
I stored away and used to fight for life on the sandy winter beach,
if a journey ends badly it's better than no journey taken at all
and when mine finally ends I know I'll still be heading further North.

Eternity is in a million blades of grass, heaven in a chunk of ironstone
in our hands, not utopian, there are none so blind who will not see
we do not own the land, we cannot claim it as private or public property
we are made of it and return to it and all that's left is infinite energy,
not listening to it, making plants and animals things, will make all a rock
upon which nothing will be built with no builders' hands left to build,
I can talk to the impossible horizon and back but cannot say what I know
watching the non-stop happened-then, happening-now human show,
I was silent in the elevator heading down, silent for hours in the town
and the silence is the treasure that I brought down and took back home
to be examined without language in the precious moments of being alone
to be carried carefully, returned to in the minutes before words form
in emergencies of health and faith, in moments of overflow of facts,
retreated to when confronted with Brecht's wrongly named Bestial Acts.

It's quiet here on the coast now with no notes in our Teesside Requiem
no roar from the fire's furnace, no steady note of a steelworks hum,
we all mumble our mantra *the smoke in the lungs the fire in the bones:*
we used to build ships, we used to make steel, we worked the blue stone,
we have to stop and see the land below see all the people living here
alone: understand we move forward better all in difference but all as one
rather than fight like rats for the last scraps in a scraped out barrel.
I want to tell the people everywhere; consider this word: *bountiful*
it doesn't mean you should start counting and hoarding what can't be kept
its meaning is all encompassing, can only be brought about by sharing all,
dream of a new international thinking, cause the corporations to fall.
Then, I'm no preacher. I talk and I report, bear witness and sit silent
as voices rant and babble online, in parliaments, on television,
I hold in my hands no easy answers and am unsettled by any certainty,
can't fathom what is the world within and what the world without,
New Molokovian, travelling clown, pope of the church of doubt.
I have no intention of joining any party that seeks to control me
and will not start to let form or decorum make me watch my words.
I dismount the shabby Teesside train recalling Advent and Lent:
old rituals observed in a childhood shifted out of synch with time,
industrialists funded temperance and Methodist churches
on our expanding ferric frontier to keep the workers sober,
washed and so called civilised for the rigours of the daily grind.
Hungry Irish held onto Catholicism to suffer beautifully in,
left redemption urges in the weave and weft of my words,
left echoes of a rapidly ageing moral world in my time line.
We all know, began Father Brennan's shut-eyed Easter sermon,
that *men and boys unlike women do not cry, no, they do not cry.*
Candles dripped wax tears onto fingernails to be peeled off:
counting the tedious minutes as Christ was led to crucifixion.
Reflect how the church was still full then back in the early seventies
benches lined with shipbuilders, process workers, factory girls and wives.

On the way back from Siberia as winter's first bite gripped the bones
I saw a holy moment of my own that will always give me hope
in Pityak Market we wandered, ate shazlik more rat than chicken,
laughed at Finn Rock star image in the ramshackle men's toilets
wondering if whoever put it up could see the homo-erotic allure
in the bare chest stance of Ville Valo. We all felt a sense of threat
as crowds of poorly dressed kids followed us around from stall to stall,
some begging, some trying to sell us matches, eyeing up our bags,
Kalle says *perhaps it wasn't rat but human bones in that shazlik*
and we laugh and start to nervously look around in fading light,
see no authorities but Esa has no fear, his pocket bottle's lit him up
his hair is matted like Rasputin's though he's off stage the blue lights on
he wanders off up a dim path to the outer stalls where he seeks a gift
for a lady he may have a chance with back in Moscow, a mob of urchins
in his wake, we worry he won't return, lose sight of him, as the tension
hits its height he reappears with children leading him by the sleeve,
he mimes, they laugh, he goofs around with his purple poet's hat
they are are all lit up by his inner radiance. For the first time I believe
that its possible that love might save this glowing suffering man.
The thought lingers as Rita's bad water gives Kalle and me a type
of evil dysentery on the last limping leg back to the Finland Station
while Esa and Aki get robbed by bad policemen in St Petersburg,
and a world of puke shit and blood is brought to birth, I hold on
to the moment and to the thought of getting back to my daughter
and dream of the warmth of the light of my own golden woman.

I sit until the last passenger disembarks onto the concrete platform,
only minutes have passed on the mobile phone's luminous face
but we are stretched and torn in a chasm between past and present
round here too – between the age of steel and ships receding,
and an Empire falling, the advent of microchips and hypermarkets.
Cyberspace, Worldwide Web, Social Networks whirl a maelstrom,
full of claim and counterclaim, truth, lies, hate and propaganda;
the shock of my own fifty years spanning such a shift in epochs!
Shocking that this information age and cheap budget airline travel,
that sets you free from time to time, year on year, to write and wander,
has done nothing much for those people still eking out their lives
in this sprawling post-industrial landscape, despite its weird wonders.
All the money made here has left us is its lingering remnants:
in the eerie moonscape of the last smouldering slag-heap
thin shades of pale smoke trace lines in a star-filled sky,
the dead blast furnace no longer dyes the night faint amber,
meanwhile out on the salt marshes a dirty winged swan
dips his curved neck in cold water to scrape for survival;
whilst out in Siberia one of the last tigers makes a slow kill.
I soft finger the scar on my neck, contemplate life and radiation
then take a long slow sip from a hip flask; between stations.

Acknowledgements

Thanks to Mayakovsky, Mandelstam, Blake, Eisenstein and '66 Bob Dylan for existing in eternity so I could jam with them.

Some of the material in this book was adapted from shorter poems published in the pamphlet *Peripheries* co-authored with Riina Katajavuori (Ek Zuban 2006).

Thanks to Esa Hirvonen and Ville Ropponen for inviting me to Siberia and the Fenn Ugric Writer's Conference along with the Finnish delegation. I am grateful to the Russian, Khanty and Mansi people for their wonderful hospitality.

Thanks to Runoviikko and Kiila organisations in Finland and Teesside University for supporting my trips back and forth to Finland to research this book.

Thanks also to the musicians Anton Flint, Kevin Howard, Dominic Nelson Ashley, Masi Hukari and Jussi Villgren for jamming on early drafts and fragments and helping me find my rhythm in the piece.

Gratitude to Bob Beagrie for his companionship, constant example and encouragement, Andy Croft and Mark Robinson for making me believe a long poem was possible.

Special thanks to Rebecca Willoughby for being my Golden Woman.

And thanks to Kalle Niinikangas for saving my life on multiple occasions on the road of excess.